Harmony of Hearts & Artistry

Love Beyond Words

Hellen Harvey

Contents

Introduction

In a world where words and melodies waltz through life, there exists a timeless tale—a love story that transcends the boundaries of ink and the echoes of music. It's a story that begins not with a glance, but with a verse; not with a touch, but with a chord.

Meet Emily, a poet with a soul painted in the hues of words. Her verses are like a gentle dance, weaving emotions into delicate tapestries, allowing the whispers of her heart to echo through her stanzas.
And then there is Ethan, a musician with a heart strumming to the rhythm of his melodies. His music breathes life into the silent spaces, painting emotions in vibrant hues that resonate with every soul that listens.

Their paths converged in the realm of creativity, at the intersection of art and the pulse of life. Each creation, a brushstroke on the canvas of fate, brought them closer. Their art became a silent dialogue—a conversation where their hearts spoke volumes without uttering a word.
This is a story where love is not just a fleeting emotion, but a timeless masterpiece—a composition written in the language of the heart, a poetry penned in eternal ink. It's a tale of love beyond words, where art and affection harmonize, painting a love story that sings in the soul's symphony.
Join Emily and Ethan on a journey where art intertwines with love, and the unspoken becomes the sweetest melody—a journey where words are not enough, and love transcends the boundaries of language.

Characters

1. Emily Hartman

A gifted wordsmith based in New York City, known for her eloquence and grace with words. Emily is the central character in the story, guarded by past relationships but deeply passionate about her craft.

2. Ethan Reed

A charismatic musician and songwriter, also based in New York City. Ethan is drawn to Emily's literary charm and artistic prowess. He seeks solace in her words and develops a profound connection with her.

3. Natalie Turner

Emily's best friend and confidante, a fellow writer, and a source of constant support in her life. Natalie encourages Emily to embrace love again and to trust in the unspoken language of the heart.

4. Marcus Sinclair

A successful author and Emily's former love interest, whose betrayal left her guarded. His actions have influenced Emily's perspective on love and relationships.

5. Lena Adams

Emily's mentor and a well-respected poet, providing guidance and wisdom as Emily navigates the complexities of her budding romance with Ethan.

6. Mason Harper

A close friend of Ethan and a fellow musician. Mason plays a supportive role in Ethan's life and offers advice as Ethan falls for Emily.

7. Aria Martinez

A vibrant and talented artist, Emily's roommate, and close friend, who serves as a sounding board for Emily's emotional journey and budding relationship with Ethan.

Chapter 1
Ink and Heartbeats

Emily sat on a plush chair, clutching her latest poem in her hands, her heart racing as she waited for her turn to read at the crowded poetry event.

Ethan, the musician, leaned against a wall nearby, his guitar in hand, his eyes scanning the room. Catching sight of Emily, he was drawn to her presence, an inexplicable pull.

As the previous poet finished, the host introduced Emily. She stood, took a deep breath, and stepped up to the microphone. "Hello, everyone. This poem is called 'Whispers of the Soul.' "

The room fell silent, the air thick with anticipation. Ethan listened intently, captivated by the cadence of her voice and the depth of her words.

Emily continued, her voice a gentle melody, "In the quietude of midnight's embrace, whispers of the soul find their grace..."
Ethan's fingers lightly strummed his guitar, unconsciously creating a soft, accompanying tune.
Emily's eyes met Ethan's, and for a fleeting moment, their souls connected, words unnecessary to convey the spark of connection.

She concluded her poem, the room erupting in applause. As she stepped away from the microphone, Ethan approached her with a warm smile. "Your words are beautiful, like music to my ears."

Blushing, Emily replied, "Thank you. And your music felt like poetry to my heart."

Ethan extended a hand, introducing himself, "I'm Ethan, by the way. Your words really struck a chord with me."

Emily accepted his hand, a genuine smile gracing her lips. "Emily. It's a pleasure to meet you, Ethan. Your music had a similar effect on me. There's a magical synergy between words and melodies."

He nodded, enthusiasm in his eyes. "Absolutely! It's like they're two sides of the same coin, expressing what we feel in different ways."

Their conversation flowed effortlessly, like a dance of thoughts and ideas. They shared stories of their artistic journeys, their dreams, and the challenges they faced in pursuing their passions.

Emily admitted, "I sometimes struggle to find the right words for my feelings, even though words are my craft."

Ethan empathized, "I understand. Music often expresses what my heart wants to say when words fall short."

As the night continued, they found themselves lost in conversation, the world around them fading into the background. Their connection was palpable, a unique understanding that words could only attempt to encapsulate.

Emily, feeling a sense of warmth and comfort, whispered to herself, "Maybe, just maybe, this is the start of something beautiful, something beyond words."

Ethan leaned in closer, the hum of the room fading as if it was just the two of them. "You know, sometimes the best things are said without words, through a glance or a melody."

Emily nodded, her eyes holding a spark of understanding. "I couldn't agree more. It's like finding a silent resonance, an unspoken connection."

As the night wore on, they discovered shared interests and kindred spirits in each other. Ethan revealed his love for late-night strolls in the city, and Emily confessed her fascination with starlit skies.
"We should go for a midnight walk sometime, "Ethan suggested, a playful glint in his eyes.
"I'd like that, "Emily replied, a blush tinting her cheeks.

Their conversation deepened, exploring life, dreams, and the small wonders that often go unnoticed.

Ethan found himself captivated not only by Emily's words but by the genuine person she was.

Before parting ways, he said, "Emily, I hope our paths cross again. There's something extraordinary about meeting someone who speaks to your soul."
Emily smiled, her heart echoing his sentiments. "I believe in fate. Maybe our meeting was destined."

As they exchanged contact information, they both knew this encounter was the beginning of a beautiful journey, one that would be written not just in words but in the silent promises of the heart.

Chapter 2
Chance Encounter

The city lights danced in the night sky as Emily and Ethan found themselves at a quaint café, seated across from each other.
Ethan grinned, stirring his coffee. "Fancy meeting you again so soon. It's like destiny has its own plans."

Emily chuckled, "Indeed, fate seems to be orchestrating this encounter. Perhaps our muses are conspiring as well."

Their laughter filled the air, blending with the soft melody playing in the background.
Ethan leaned forward, his eyes curious. "Tell me, Emily, what inspires your poetry? What makes your heart sing?"

She pondered for a moment, her eyes lighting up with passion. "Life, emotions, and the beauty of the ordinary. I find inspiration in fleeting moments that often go unnoticed, but are imbued with profound meaning."

He nodded, understanding her perspective. "It's amazing how art can breathe life into the seemingly mundane."

As the evening unfolded, they shared anecdotes of their creative processes, exchanging tales of triumphs and tribulations in their respective artistic realms.
Emily confessed, "There are times when I struggle to find my voice, but meeting people like you, Ethan, reminds me of the power of genuine connection."

Ethan smiled warmly. "Likewise. Your words have a way of touching hearts, including mine."

Their conversation flowed effortlessly, a dance of intellect and emotions. In that café, amidst the soothing ambiance, they discovered a shared love for art, poetry, and the magic that could unfold when two creative souls come together.

Natalie, Emily's best friend and fellow writer, joined them at the café, her eyes sparkling with excitement. "Emily, Ethan, fate must be a fan of collaborations. Meeting again so soon!"

Ethan grinned, extending a hand. "I'm Ethan, a musician. Pleasure to meet you, Natalie."

Natalie shook his hand, her enthusiasm infectious. "Likewise! I've heard wonderful things about your music."

As they all settled into conversation, sharing stories and laughter, the energy at the table buzzed with creativity.

Natalie turned to Ethan, curious. "So, Ethan, what inspires your music? Is it similar to Emily's poetic inspiration?"

Ethan nodded, thoughtful. "In a way, yes. Emotions, life experiences, and the ebb and flow of the world around us fuel my music. It's an expression of the unseen and the unspoken."

Emily chimed in, "It's beautiful how art can transcend mediums yet remain connected through the depth of emotions."

Their exchange of ideas and artistic philosophies continued, weaving a tapestry of creativity and mutual understanding.

Aria, Emily's roommate and a talented artist, also joined, completing the quartet of creative minds. "Emily, Ethan, I've been eavesdropping on your conversation. It's inspiring to witness the birth of artistic connections."

Ethan smiled warmly, appreciating the sentiment. "Thank you, Aria. Art has a way of bringing kindred souls together."

In that cozy café, the four creatives found a unique camaraderie, a bond formed not only by fate but also by the magic that art and creativity could manifest.

As the evening progressed, their conversation deepened, exploring not only their artistic endeavors but also their personal dreams and desires.
Natalie leaned forward, her eyes alight with curiosity. "So, Emily, where do you see your poetry taking you in the future?"

Emily considered the question, her gaze turning introspective. "I dream of publishing a collection of my poems, reaching people on a broader scale, and perhaps inspiring them to find solace or joy in my words."
Ethan chimed in, "That's a beautiful aspiration. I believe your words have the power to touch many hearts."

Encouraged by their genuine interest, Emily turned the conversation toward Ethan. "And what about you, Ethan? What's your musical journey's destination?"

Ethan grinned, his passion evident. "I want to create music that resonates with people, that becomes a soundtrack to their lives. Every chord, every lyric, a piece of my soul connecting with theirs."

Aria, the artist, added her perspective, "It's incredible how art allows us to leave a piece of ourselves in the world, a mark of our existence."

In that lively exchange of dreams and aspirations, they found kindred spirits who understood the urge to create, to express, and to be heard.

As the night drew to a close, they made plans to attend a local art exhibit, a blend of their worlds colliding once again. They parted ways, hearts brimming with inspiration and the promise of more chance encounters.

Chapter 3
Whispers of the Soul

Emily stood at her writing desk, surrounded by notebooks and pens, her mind lost in the labyrinth of her thoughts.
Ethan's text notification broke her concentration. "Hey, Emily! How about a walk in the park and some live music later?"

She smiled, typing her response. "Sounds perfect. The park always seems to have whispers of inspiration."
They met at the park, the air crisp with the promise of autumn. A soft melody played on Ethan's acoustic guitar, blending seamlessly with the rustling leaves.

Emily found a peaceful spot, gazing at the pond, lost in the rhythm of Ethan's music. "Your melodies, Ethan, they weave stories of their own."

Ethan played a gentle tune, his eyes reflecting the sincerity of his craft. "And your words, Emily, they breathe life into those stories."

They shared an understanding, a silent acknowledgment of the connection between their art forms.

Natalie, joining them at the park, sat down and said, "It's amazing how your creativity complements each other. A beautiful symbiosis."
Ethan nodded, strumming a chord. "Indeed, it's like our art forms are engaged in a never-ending dance."

As the sun set, painting the sky with hues of orange and pink, Emily recited one of her recent poems inspired by the moment, her voice adding a poignant layer to the ambiance.

In that golden hour, surrounded by nature's canvas and the echoes of their creativity, they realized that the beauty of their artistic connection surpassed even their wildest dreams.

Ethan continued to play, the melodies caressing the air, echoing Emily's emotions. Natalie, always a keen observer, couldn't help but comment, "It's like your music amplifies the soul of Emily's poetry."

Emily smiled appreciatively, her eyes reflecting gratitude. "Yes, Ethan has a remarkable ability to give life to the silent verses of my poems."

Ethan acknowledged the connection, his eyes locked on Emily. "Your words provide the canvas; I merely add the strokes of music to complete the masterpiece."
Aria, who had joined them as well, chimed in, "It's beautiful to witness how your creativity flourishes when intertwined."

In that moment, they shared an unspoken understanding—an unbreakable bond forged through their shared love for art and expression.
As the day turned into night, they decided to continue their creative adventure at a nearby café. The warmth of the café and the aroma of coffee set the perfect

atmosphere for them to delve deeper into discussions about their creative endeavors.

Ethan, setting his guitar aside for a moment, said, "I feel that our art forms are like languages of the soul, each expressing emotions in its unique way."

Natalie added, "And when those languages converge, they create a symphony of emotions that resonate with everyone."

In the heart of the café, amidst the hum of conversations and the aroma of freshly brewed coffee, they realized that their artistic connection wasn't just a chance encounter— it was a harmonious fusion of their souls.

Ethan's fingers gently caressed the strings of his guitar, like a painter delicately applying brushstrokes to a canvas. Each chord resonated with the surroundings, painting the air with musical hues.

Emily, in her element, stood amidst the gentle breeze, her long hair gently swaying like golden tendrils as if mirroring the dance of autumn leaves. Her words floated on the air, leaving behind an ethereal trail of emotions.

Natalie observed, captivated by the scene before her. She saw Ethan's music as a river, carving its course through the landscape, and Emily's words as the gentle rain, nourishing the earth of their creative collaboration.

Aria, the artist among them, visualized the melodies as vibrant strokes of paint on an invisible canvas, merging with the words like hues blending seamlessly in a masterpiece.

The sun dipped below the horizon, casting the world in twilight hues—ambers, pinks, and purples. The park transformed into a realm of artistic enchantment, where poetry, music, and nature danced in harmony.

In the café, the flickering candlelight painted shadows on the walls, creating a cozy sanctuary. The aroma of coffee intermingled with the scent of ink from Emily's open notebook, forming an olfactory tapestry of their creative sanctuary.

As they conversed, their words took on a visual quality, weaving a tapestry of ideas and visions, much like brushstrokes on the canvas of their shared artistic journey.

Chapter 4
Melodies of the Heart

Emily sat on a weathered bench near the city's bustling square, the notes of Ethan's guitar floating through the air, painting the busy street with a tranquil melody.

Ethan strummed the strings, his eyes closed, lost in the music. "Sometimes, I feel like music is the heart's unspoken language. It speaks what words often fail to convey."

She nodded in agreement, her eyes reflecting the sincerity of his sentiment. "And your melodies touch the heart in a way that's both profound and comforting."

A passerby stopped to listen, momentarily captivated by the musical serenade, a testament to the power of Ethan's art.

Ethan smiled, opening his eyes to meet Emily's gaze. "Much like your poetry, Emily. It has a way of reaching into the depths of the soul."

Emboldened by the compliment, Emily shared, "Your music inspired my latest poem. It danced in my mind, and the words simply flowed."

He leaned closer, their connection palpable. "I'm honored to have played a part in inspiring your beautiful words."

In that moment, amidst the city's symphony and the shared appreciation of their crafts, they realized that their art not only fueled their passion but also deepened their connection—a bond woven from the threads of music and poetry.

The sun began to set, casting a warm, golden glow over the scene. Ethan played a softer tune, the melody a tender caress against the backdrop of the approaching night.

Emily, her heart moved by the music, whispered, "It's like your guitar is speaking the language of emotions, telling stories that resonate within."
Ethan nodded, the corners of his lips curled into a gentle smile. "And your poetry, Emily, is like a dance of words, painting pictures in the mind and stirring the heart."

Their exchange was like a duet, each note and word harmoniously complementing the other.
As the music gently faded, they sat in companionable silence, the city lights beginning to illuminate the surroundings. The transition from day to night mirrored the evolving cadence of their budding relationship.

Natalie, always perceptive, noted the unspoken connection between them. "Your artistic synergy is truly magical. It's like you complete each other's artistic sentences."

Aria, the artist, added, "It's as if your creativity merges into a symphony of art, a masterpiece in the making."
In that tranquil moment, they embraced the profound understanding that they were more than two artists— they were soulmates in the realm of art and love.

Ethan looked at Emily, his eyes reflecting a question he had been pondering. "Emily, do you think art, our art, has a way of bringing people closer, of fostering connections?"

She contemplated his question, her gaze fixed on the distant horizon. "Absolutely. Art is a universal language, transcending boundaries and touching the very essence of humanity. It allows us to connect on a deeper level, to understand and be understood."

He nodded, appreciating her perspective. "It's fascinating how a single chord or a carefully chosen word can evoke emotions that resonate universally. Art has this incredible power to unite."

Emily added, "And in this union, we find something extraordinary. It's not just the art—it's the connection it creates the bonds it forms."

Their thoughts merged, weaving a beautiful dialogue that underscored their shared understanding of art's profound impact on their lives and the world around them.
As the night enveloped the city, Ethan gently broke the silence, his voice tender. "Emily, this connection we share through our art—it's something special, isn't it?"

She smiled, her eyes reflecting the city lights. "Indeed, it's like our hearts beat to the same rhythm, creating a melody that resonates within us."

In that moment, their hearts acknowledged a deeper truth: their artistic connection was not just a fleeting encounter but the beginning of a timeless love story.

Ethan leaned closer, his gaze gentle yet intense. "Emily, have you ever felt that art is a mirror to our souls, reflecting our innermost feelings and desires?"

Emily met his gaze, the sincerity in his eyes echoing her own sentiments. "Absolutely. It's like art gives voice to the silent parts of our being, revealing what we sometimes struggle to say."

Their connection deepened, their hearts beating in unison with the rhythm of their artistic passions.
He continued, "And when our art intertwines, it's like a beautiful dance, each note and word harmonizing perfectly."

She nodded, her expression thoughtful. "It's as if our creativity is entwined by an invisible thread, guiding us to create something meaningful together."

In the quietude of that moment, they realized that their artistic connection was akin to a duet—a symphony where their souls played the music of love.
As the night embraced them, Ethan whispered, "Emily, I believe our art has a destiny of its own, a journey waiting to unfold."

She smiled, her heart echoing his belief. "Yes, a destiny written in melodies and verses, uniting our hearts in an everlasting song."

In that serenade of the night, they discovered a promise—
the promise of an artistic love that would compose a
beautiful, timeless melody.

Chapter 5
Written in the Stars

Emily and Ethan found themselves on a rooftop, the city's lights painting the sky with a tapestry of twinkling stars. The magic of the night seemed to breathe life into their budding love.

Ethan broke the silence, his words reflecting the wonder of the moment. "It's as if the stars are witness to our journey, illuminating our path forward."

Emily, lost in the celestial beauty, nodded in agreement. "Yes, like they're whispering tales of love and destiny, painting constellations in our honor."

He took her hand, the warmth of their connection palpable in the cool night air. "Emily, do you believe in fate, that our meeting was written in the stars?"

Her eyes held a spark of belief. "I do. It's like the universe conspired to bring two creative souls together, entwining our paths."

They gazed at the night sky, feeling the cosmic embrace of destiny guiding their hearts.
Ethan softly said, "I've always believed that our art leads us to where we're meant to be, like the strokes of a brush guiding a masterpiece."
Emily smiled, feeling the truth in his words. "Our art has been our compass, leading us to this moment, written in the stars."

In that celestial serenity, they realized that their love story was part of a grander cosmic design, a masterpiece painted by the universe, and they were merely the willing artists.

Chapter 6
Silent Confessions

Amidst the soft glow of candlelight in a cozy café, Emily and Ethan found themselves in a corner, their hearts brimming with unspoken affection.

Ethan looked at Emily, his eyes a reflection of his emotions. "Emily, there's something I've wanted to tell you for a while now."

She met his gaze, her heart fluttering with anticipation. "What is it, Ethan?"
He took a deep breath, his voice a gentle caress. "Every note I play every melody I create—it's a silent confession of my love for you."

A soft gasp escaped her lips, her eyes glistening with emotion. "Ethan, I feel the same way. Every poem I write every word I choose—it's an expression of my love for you."

In that moment, time seemed to stand still as their unspoken feelings wove an invisible bond, stronger than any words could convey.

Ethan reached for her hand, the touch comforting and electrifying. "Emily, our hearts beat in harmony, playing the most beautiful love song. Can you hear it too?"
Her smile was like a sunrise, warming his soul. "Yes, Ethan. Our love is a silent melody that echoes in the chambers of our hearts."

As the evening embraced them, they sat in the quietude of love, basking in the silent confessions that spoke louder than any words ever could.

Ethan leaned closer, their hands entwined, his voice a gentle whisper. "I've waited for the perfect moment to express what's in my heart, but I realize every moment with you is perfect."

Emily felt a rush of emotion, her heart soaring. "Ethan, you've painted colors in my world I never knew existed. Your music has filled the silent gaps in my soul."

Their eyes locked, speaking volumes without words—a language only they understood.
He continued, "Emily, you're the poetry of my melodies, the essence of every song I play."
She touched his cheek tenderly, her voice soft but resolute. "And you, Ethan, are the rhythm of my heart, the inspiration behind every verse I write."

In that intimate space, they knew their love was a symphony—a beautiful composition that would resonate through the chapters of their lives.

As the night deepened and the world outside disappeared, they savored the silent confessions that bound their hearts in an unbreakable bond.

Ethan brushed a lock of hair from Emily's face, his eyes tender and earnest. "Emily, every time I play my guitar, it's as if my heart is serenading you, expressing what words fail to capture."

Emily's gaze was unwavering, her voice filled with emotion. "Ethan, your music has breathed life into my words, elevating them to a dance of emotions. It's like you've found the melody to my soul."

He traced circles with his thumb on her palm, the connection palpable. "I believe in the unspoken language of love—the way our hearts beat in sync, conveying what no words can."

Emily smiled, her heart singing. "Yes, Ethan, it's like our souls converse in a beautiful silence, an eternal dialogue that needs no translation."

In that sacred moment, amidst the quiet intimacy of the café, they realized that their love was a story written in the pauses, the unsung notes—a story told by the spaces between their heartbeats.

Chapter 7
Love Resonance

The morning sun painted the sky in hues of pink and gold as Emily, Ethan, Natalie, and Aria sat in a sunlit room, sipping coffee and sharing their dreams.

Natalie, her eyes bright with excitement, said, "I've been thinking—what if we organize an event where Emily's poetry and Ethan's music take center stage? A night of pure artistic fusion."

Ethan's face lit up with enthusiasm. "That's a fantastic idea! A night where our art forms merge into one beautiful performance."

Emily nodded in agreement, her heart eager to embrace this opportunity. "It would be like our love for art resonating through the night, a melody that speaks to every soul."

Aria, always the creative visionary, added, "We could incorporate visuals, too—my paintings could be the backdrop, bringing an immersive experience."

In that moment, a dream was born—a dream to create an event that would not only showcase their talents but also celebrate their artistic connection.

As they brainstormed ideas and shared their visions, they realized that their love for art was not only about creating but also about sharing, touching hearts, and leaving an indelible mark on the world.

Ethan leaned back, a smile playing on his lips. "Imagine the melodies blending seamlessly with Emily's poignant poetry, accompanied by the strokes of Aria's brush on canvas. It would be a masterpiece in motion."

Emily added, her eyes alight with excitement, "And the emotions in our art would speak to the audience, telling a story that transcends words or notes."

Natalie chimed in, "We could invite other artists, too—dancers, actors. A true celebration of creativity and expression."

Aria, envisioning the event, exclaimed, "The stage will be alive with passion and energy. The fusion of our art will create a resonance that lingers in people's hearts."

Their collective enthusiasm fueled the dream, and they began planning the event, each person contributing their unique perspective, shaping what would be a night to remember.

In that room, amidst the chatter and laughter, they realized that their friendship and shared love for art were the catalysts for something truly extraordinary—an artistic collaboration that would resonate beyond the walls of the venue.
Ethan leaned forward, his eyes reflecting the sincerity of his words. "Art is our essence, the heartbeat of our souls. It's the language we speak when our hearts overflow."

Emily nodded in agreement, her passion evident in her voice. "Art is the sanctuary where we find solace, the canvas where we pour our emotions, the melody that comforts our spirits."

Natalie joined in, her conviction unwavering. "It's the conduit through which we communicate the depths of our being, transcending boundaries and touching lives."

Aria added, her artistic spirit shining through, "Art is the reflection of humanity's collective soul, a tapestry woven with threads of creativity and love."

In that moment, their sincerity echoed through the room—a chorus of voices united by their unwavering belief in the transformative power of art.

Together, they envisioned a world where their shared love for art would ripple through generations, leaving an indelible mark on the fabric of human experience.

Chapter 8
Eternal Ink

Emily and Ethan found themselves in a cozy bookstore, surrounded by the comforting scent of old books and the promise of new stories.

Ethan picked up a book, a smile playing on his lips. "There's something magical about the written word. It's like ink on paper becomes a gateway to another world."

Emily nodded, sharing his sentiment. "Indeed. Every page turned is a step into a different adventure, a new perspective."

As they explored the bookstore, their fingers tracing the spines of countless volumes, Emily's eyes fell on a book of poetry. She picked it up, her heart stirred by the verses.

Ethan, seeing her expression, asked, "What caught your eye?"

Emily read a line aloud, her voice infused with the poet's emotion. "Ink stains of the heart, forever etched in time."

Ethan smiled, understanding the depth of those words. "It's like our art—forever imprinted on the canvas of existence, leaving a mark beyond our years."

Their connection deepened as they discussed their love for literature, art, and the beauty of eternal ink that bound their souls.

In the embrace of books and poetry, they realized that their love, too, was like eternal ink—forever etched in the pages of their hearts.

Ethan picked up another book, an anthology of love poems. "Love in words—it's like capturing a piece of the heart's melody and preserving it for eternity."

Emily, captivated by his words, shared her thoughts, "And art is an ode to that melody, painting its hues and nuances, making it visible to the world."
Their dialogue turned into a dance of ideas, twirling around the essence of art and love.

Ethan leaned closer, his eyes intense. "Emily, you've given my music a voice—a language that speaks volumes of love and emotions."

She touched his arm gently, moved by his sincerity. "And you, Ethan, have breathed life into my poetry, turning ink and paper into a symphony of feelings."

In that bookstore, amidst the shelves adorned with literary masterpieces, they realized that their artistic connection was a treasure—words and notes that would stand the test of time.

Their love story was like a book, each chapter written with the ink of their hearts, leaving an imprint for generations to read and be inspired.
Ethan gently caressed the spine of a well-worn book, a thoughtful expression on his face. "Books hold memories—whispers of the past, dreams of the future. They're a testament to the endurance of human thought and emotion."

Emily traced the bookshelves, her eyes bright with passion. "Much like our art, the essence of humanity is captured in poems and melodies. It's the beating heart of creativity."

He nodded, sharing her enthusiasm. "Our journey in art—it's like turning the pages of a book, each stroke and stanza revealing a new facet of our souls."

Emily's gaze met his, a profound connection sparking between them. "And just as every word in a book matters, every note in a melody holds significance. Our art is a story, waiting to be read and heard."

In that haven of literature and art, surrounded by the whispers of literary greats and the promise of their own creative destiny, they realized their love for each other was a narrative—a tale that would resonate through the ages.

In the soft glow of twilight, atop a hill overlooking the city, Emily and Ethan stood hand in hand, the city lights shimmering below them.

Ethan gazed into Emily's eyes, his voice a whisper of love. "Emily, from the very first note, you've been the melody of my heart, the symphony of my soul."
Tears of joy glistened in Emily's eyes. "And you, Ethan, have been the poetry in my veins, the verse that completes my story."

He dropped to one knee, a ring in his hand, the symbol of their love. "Emily, will you be the harmony to my music, the forever to my song?"

With a heart overflowing with love, she nodded, tears of happiness cascading down her cheeks. "Yes, Ethan, a thousand times yes."

Their embrace was a celebration of love, a dance of hearts that had found their perfect rhythm.
In that magical moment, amidst the whispers of the wind and the city's gentle hum, they knew their love was a masterpiece—an everlasting composition written in the language of love, a story woven through ink and heartbeats.

And as they stood there, their love echoing through the night, they realized that in the world of art and love, theirs was a tale for the ages—an eternal symphony.

Epilogue
The Written Future

The sun dipped below the horizon, painting the sky with hues of orange and pink, casting a soft, golden light across the city.

Years had passed since that moment on the hill, where Emily and Ethan had exchanged their vows of love. Now, their journey as husband and wife had transformed into a beautiful symphony, a melody written in the pages of their life together.

They had embraced their dreams, crafting a life that celebrated their art and their love. Their collaborative event, "Artistic Fusion, "had become an annual affair, a night where artists of all kinds gathered to share their love for creativity.

Natalie had pursued her passion for photography, capturing the world's moments in a lens that revealed both heart and soul.

Aria's paintings had graced galleries and museums, each stroke of her brush telling a story of emotions and colors. And amidst the hustle and bustle of their creative endeavors, Emily and Ethan had carved moments of quiet love, painting their own canvas of intimacy and affection.

As they stood on their balcony, the city lights twinkling below, they knew their story was still being written—an ever-evolving poem of love and art.

Together, they faced the unwritten future, their hearts and hands intertwined, ready to compose a melody that would resonate for generations to come.

And in that love-filled moment, they whispered to the night, "To love, to art, and to the endless possibilities of our unwritten future."

Book Synopsis

In the bustling heart of New York City, amidst the clatter of ambition and dreams, lives the enigmatic Emily Hartman, a gifted wordsmith who pours her heart into crafting beautiful poems and prose. Her eloquence and grace with words have earned her acclaim, but her heart remains guarded, scarred by past relationships. Enter Ethan Reed, a charismatic musician seeking solace from the cacophony of fame. Drawn to Emily's literary charm, Ethan finds himself enchanted not only by her words but by the woman behind them.

Their worlds collide in a whirlwind of shared dreams and whispered confessions, the silent language of their hearts weaving a love story that transcends mere words. As Emily and Ethan navigate the intricacies of love, they discover that sometimes, emotions speak louder than syllables, and actions convey what words cannot.

"Love Beyond Words" is a tender exploration of the power of love to break down barriers, proving that in matters of the heart, sometimes silence can be the most profound expression of all. *Will Emily and Ethan find the courage to let love surpass the boundaries of language and embrace a future written in the ink of their hearts?*

www.ingramcontent.com/pod-product-compliance
Lightning Source LLC
Chambersburg PA
CBHW072218290526
45794CB00007B/2790